He has two toes on his front feet.

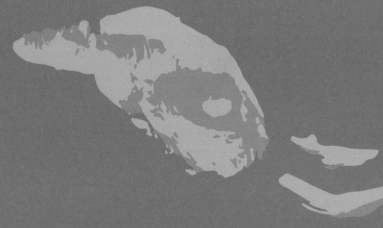

Sloths use their claws to hang from trees.

Teaching Tornero

The True Story of a Sloth Superstar

by Georgeanne Irvine

San Diego Zoo
Wildlife Alliance
Press

Teaching Tornero: The True Story of a Sloth Superstar was published by San Diego Zoo Wildlife Alliance Press in association with Blue Sneaker Press. Through these publishing efforts, we seek to inspire children and adults to care about wildlife, the natural world, and conservation.

San Diego Zoo Wildlife Alliance is a nonprofit international conservation leader, committed to inspiring a passion for nature and working toward a world where all life thrives. It supports cutting-edge conservation, and its work extends from San Diego to eco-regional conservation "hubs" across the globe.

Paul Baribault, President and Chief Executive Officer
Shawn Dixon, Chief Operating Officer
David Miller, Chief Marketing Officer
Lianne Hedditch, Vice President of Communications
Georgeanne Irvine, Director of Publishing
San Diego Zoo Wildlife Alliance
P.O. Box 120551
San Diego, CA 92112-0551
sdzwa.org | 619-231-1515

San Diego Zoo Wildlife Alliance's publishing partner is Blue Sneaker Press, an imprint of Southwestern Publishing House, Inc., 2451 Atrium Way, Nashville, TN 37214. Southwestern Publishing House is a wholly owned subsidiary of Southwestern Family of Companies, Nashville, Tennessee.

Christopher G. Capen, President, Southwestern Publishing House
Carrie Hasler, Publisher, Blue Sneaker Press
Kristin Connelly, Managing Editor
Lori Sandstrom, Art Director/Graphic Designer
swpublishinghouse.com | 800-358-0560

ISBN: 978-1-943198-17-7
Library of Congress Control Number: 2022914081
Printed in China
10 9 8 7 6 5 4 3 2 1

To Tornero, who won my heart the first time I met him, and to other wildlife ambassadors, who help inspire people to protect our planet's wild places and animals.

Acknowledgments

MY SINCEREST THANKS TO THE FOLLOWING PEOPLE FOR HELPING TO BRING TORNERO'S HEARTWARMING STORY TO LIFE:

Wildlife Connections/Wegeforth Bowl Team: Katie Springer, Kelly Salamone, Kristi Dovich, Carlee Westbrook, Julia Mehaffey, Shauna Neal, Melisa Knight, Kyle Legoll, Alison Holland, and Jessica Karsh; Wildlife Explorers Basecamp Team: Clint Lusardi, Jaimee Lafleur, Kelly Lee, Katie Miller, Kristen Craig, Kym Janke, Jessica Watters, and Tiffany Haskard; Nicki Boyd; Meg Sutherland-Smith, DVM; Carrie Hasler; Lori Sandstrom; Kristin Connelly; Angel Chambosse; David Miller; Lianne Hedditch; Bill O'Donnell; Andrew James; Darla Davis; Jenny Mehlow; Lisa Biasillo; Joy Love; Lisa Bissi; Jennifer MacEwen; Tammy Spratt; Ken Bohn; Kim Turner; and Shelley Weiss.

Special thanks to Ernest and Evelyn Rady
for their generous support of the Wildlife Ambassador Program at the San Diego Zoo.

PHOTO CREDITS:
Ken Bohn: title page, 4, 6, 7, 8, 10, 14 upper, 18, 19, 25 upper, 27 left insets, 32, 33, 34 left inset.
Georgeanne Irvine: front and back covers, front jacket flap, 3, 9, 11, 12, 13, 14 lower, 16, 17, 20, 21, 22, 23, 24, 25 lower, 26, 27 lower right, 30, 31, 34 top right. **Jaimee Lafleur:** 5 lower. **Shelley Weiss:** 15. **Melisa Knight:** 28.
Katie Springer: 29. **Darla Davis:** back jacket flap. **Minden Pictures—Suzi Eszterhas:** 34 right inset, lower right; 35 both center insets; **Pete Oxford:** 36 upper. **Shutterstock:** 34 lower left; 35 upper left and right, lower right, far right inset; 36 lower. **Dreamstime:** 34 upper left; 35 left inset, lower left, upper center.

A Sloth Surprise!

The early morning sun was just beginning to shine on the San Diego Zoo when wildlife care specialist Sonia arrived at work. She helped care for animals that were going to live at Wildlife Explorers Basecamp, an area being built where people would learn about wildlife and their habitats. When Sonia stopped by to check on Xena (Zee-na) the two-toed sloth, she was still sound asleep at the top of her habitat. Sonia could only see Xena's arms and legs hanging down because the sloth was so high.

Xena

Sloths typically have one baby at a time; twins are rare.

To get a closer look, Sonia climbed a ladder and peeked at the sleeping sloth. What she saw made her gasp: a newborn baby sloth was clinging tightly to Xena's fur. "Hey, everyone, get over here," Sonia called out to her coworkers. "You'll never guess what I just discovered."

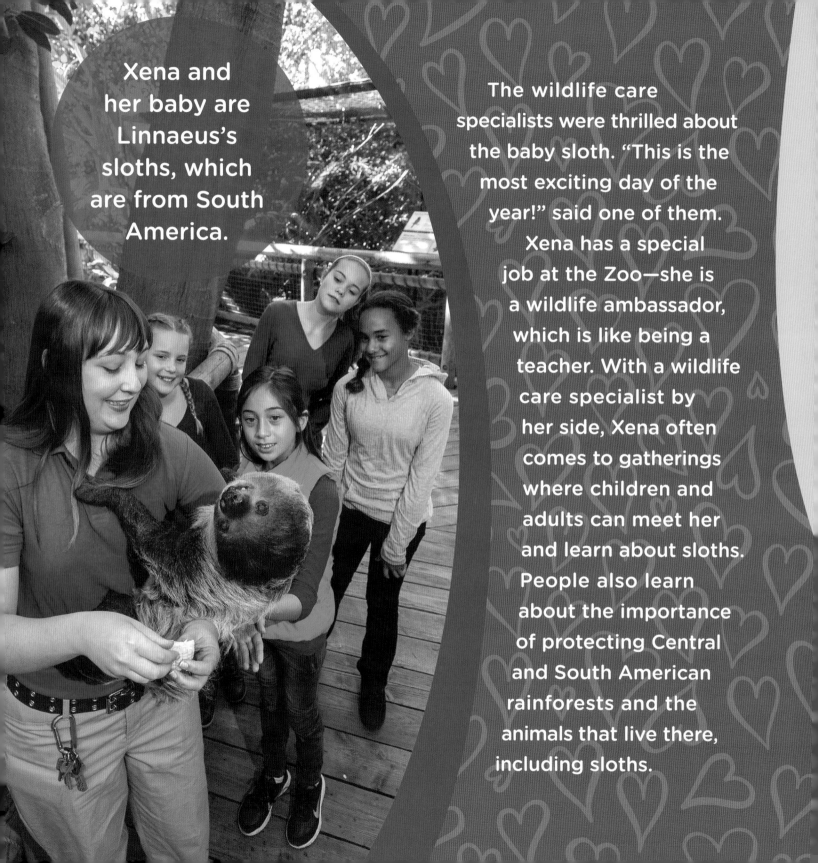

Xena and her baby are Linnaeus's sloths, which are from South America.

The wildlife care specialists were thrilled about the baby sloth. "This is the most exciting day of the year!" said one of them. Xena has a special job at the Zoo—she is a wildlife ambassador, which is like being a teacher. With a wildlife care specialist by her side, Xena often comes to gatherings where children and adults can meet her and learn about sloths. People also learn about the importance of protecting Central and South American rainforests and the animals that live there, including sloths.

When Xena was being raised by her mother, she learned from her wildlife care specialists to be an ambassador. And that was the hope for Xena's baby: while Xena raised her baby, the caregivers would teach the little sloth to become a wildlife ambassador.

But for now, Xena needed to rest and bond with her infant.

The Baby Up Close

At first, the wildlife care specialists kept an eye on Xena and her infant from afar. It was important to make sure the new mom was caring for her baby. They also wanted to see that the newborn was nursing. Xena's milk would help the baby grow and get stronger.

Brad Pitt

When the tiny sloth was a week old, the caregivers were able to get a close-up look at it. Xena let them hold her and the baby, who calmly clung to her long fur. The infant sloth had golden hair on its back, just like its dad, who was named Brad Pitt after the famous movie star.

The wildlife care specialists couldn't tell whether the baby was a boy or a girl because the sloth was so young and small. Until they knew if it was a male or female, they decided to call it Nugget.

Weighing In

When the tiny sloth was 10 days old, it was weighed for the first time. The baby clung to a soft blanket while it was on the scale. It didn't mind being away from its mom Xena for a few minutes. Nugget's weight was already over a pound, and the infant was growing larger every day.

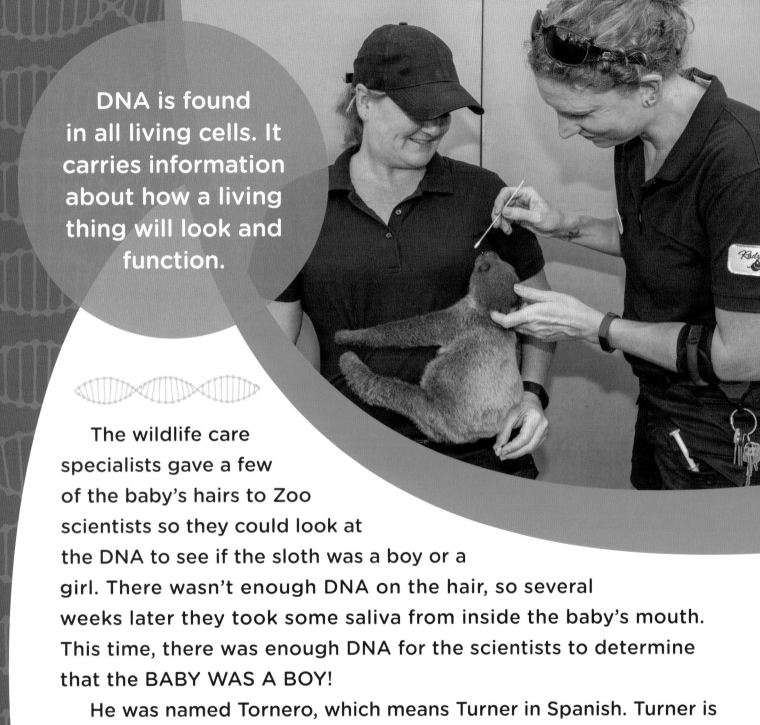

DNA is found in all living cells. It carries information about how a living thing will look and function.

The wildlife care specialists gave a few of the baby's hairs to Zoo scientists so they could look at the DNA to see if the sloth was a boy or a girl. There wasn't enough DNA on the hair, so several weeks later they took some saliva from inside the baby's mouth. This time, there was enough DNA for the scientists to determine that the BABY WAS A BOY!

He was named Tornero, which means Turner in Spanish. Turner is the last name of a generous person who donated money to the Zoo to help animals.

The Good Eater

When Tornero was first born, he nursed from his mother throughout the day. He started to nibble on bits of solid food—like apple and jicama—when he was only 10 days old. By the time Tornero was a month old, he stopped nursing and ate only fruits, vegetables, and leaves, just like sloth babies in the wild.

Like other sloths, Tornero and Xena sleep about 10–15 hours a day.

The wildlife care specialists gave Tornero broccoli, which he liked very much. Xena had never been fond of broccoli, but once Tornero started eating it, so did she! Tornero also loved bananas, but his mom never learned to like them. If a banana even touched Xena's food, she wouldn't eat any of it.

Learning to Be a Wildlife Ambassador

By the time Tornero was a few weeks old, he was already interested in interacting with his wildlife care specialists. He would shift himself around on his mother's body to get closer to them.

Sloth ambassadors play a crucial role in inspiring people to care about sloths and other wildlife.

Xena was a laid-back mother who was calm and comfortable being around people. When wildlife care specialists carried Xena from her habitat to meet and greet Zoo guests who would learn about sloths, Tornero rode along on her chest. This helped Tornero get used to new sights, sounds, and smells. And because Xena was relaxed in those situations, Tornero was relaxed, too. As he got a little older, Tornero didn't mind being carried separately from his mom.

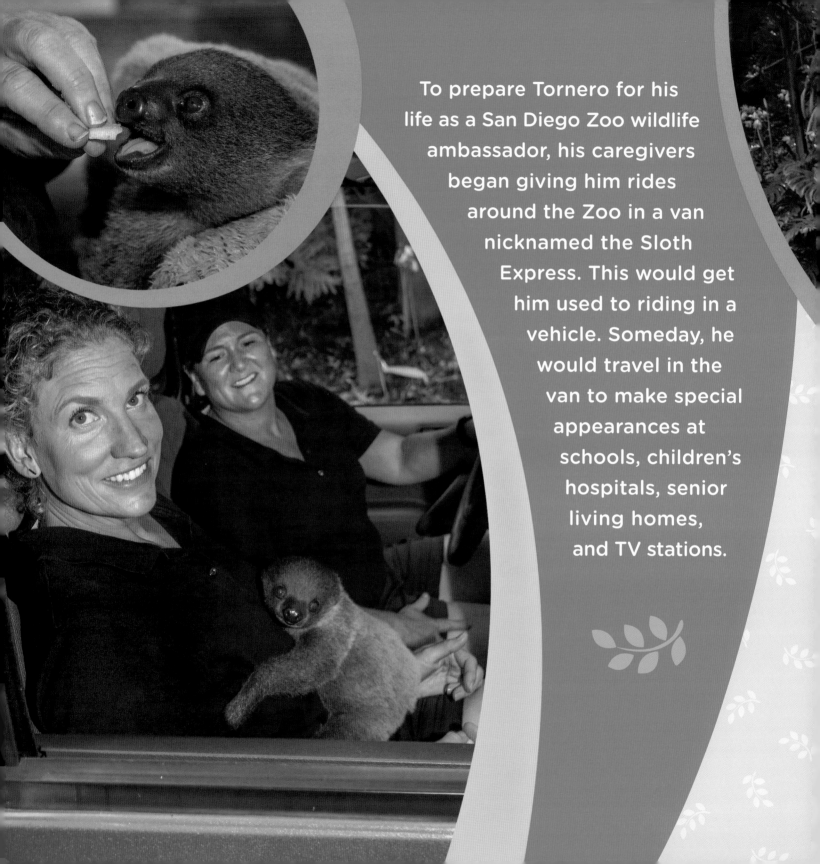

To prepare Tornero for his life as a San Diego Zoo wildlife ambassador, his caregivers began giving him rides around the Zoo in a van nicknamed the Sloth Express. This would get him used to riding in a vehicle. Someday, he would travel in the van to make special appearances at schools, children's hospitals, senior living homes, and TV stations.

For his first trip through the Zoo, he clung to a wildlife care specialist while another one drove them past the flamingos, down a canyon by the tigers, and up the hill near the penguins. Once in a while, they stopped so curious Tornero could meet a Zoo worker.

When Tornero arrived back home, a wildlife care specialist called out to Xena, who climbed down from her hammock. Then Xena stretched out so the caregiver could place Tornero on her chest, where he snuggled into her shaggy fur.

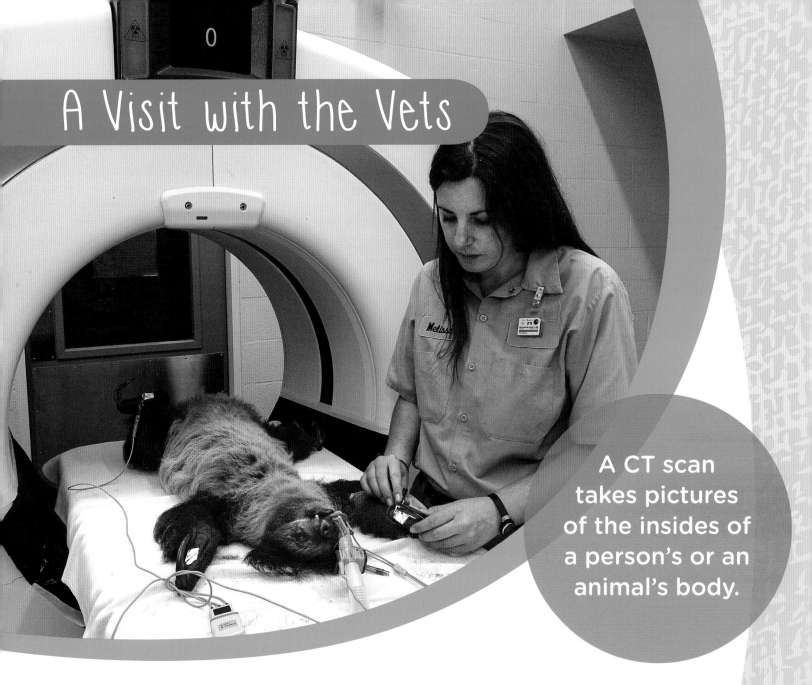

A Visit with the Vets

A CT scan takes pictures of the insides of a person's or an animal's body.

On a warm fall morning when Tornero was five months old, the wildlife care specialists noticed that Xena had a runny nose. They took her to the Zoo hospital and brought Tornero, too, so he could have a checkup.

At the hospital, Xena was given medicine to make her go to sleep. This would make it easier for the veterinarians to examine her. Using a CT scan, the vets looked at Xena's head, chest, and belly, which showed everything was normal. They also looked inside Xena's nose and took a blood test. They discovered Xena had a mild infection. So, they gave her medicine, which eventually made Xena well again.

When it was Tornero's turn, the veterinarians listened to his heart and lungs and looked in his nose, mouth, and ears. He was a healthy baby sloth! Tornero was also vaccinated to prevent a disease that can make sloths very sick.

Tornero's Big Adventure

A week after Tornero's medical checkup, wildlife care specialists took him on his biggest adventure yet: to a gigantic warehouse where lots of friendly Zoo employees were waiting to greet him. The visit would help Tornero get used to meeting new people. This was the next step in teaching him how to be a wildlife ambassador.

The warehouse is where all of the items—like plush animals, T-shirts, and toys—are stored before they are sold in Zoo and Safari Park gift shops.

For the 20-mile journey, Tornero rode safely in the back of the Sloth Express in a transport carrier, snuggling a burlap pillow. When they arrived, caregiver Kelly held Tornero and talked about sloths as the Zoo workers took photos. Tornero was so relaxed that he almost fell asleep in Kelly's arms. Before Tornero headed back to the Zoo with the wildlife care specialists, he was given a gift: a soft plush sloth that he could cling to when he wasn't with his mother.

Tornero the TV Star!

When Tornero was six months old, he visited a local television station for the first time. There, he appeared live on the Zoo Day segment of the midday news with wildlife care specialists Katie and Julia.

While he waited for his turn to be on TV, Tornero yawned, napped, and then snacked on jicama and protein biscuits. Finally, the director called out, "You're on after the commercial break. Please head to the set."

With the cameras rolling, the news anchors asked Katie and Julia questions about sloths, so viewers could learn about them. Tornero calmly hugged his burlap pillow, munching on a yellow hibiscus flower. When the show was over, the news anchors took a few selfies with Tornero and Katie.

A New Home Sweet Home

At this stage of Tornero's life, he and his mom, Xena, were already apart much of the time. It was now time for Tornero to have his own home.

The wildlife care team created a special sloth sanctuary for Tornero in an area called Wegeforth Bowl. It had two hammocks for sleeping, branches for climbing, special heaters to keep him warm at night, and many areas to explore. His new home was located down the hill from where Xena's new home, Wildlife Explorers Basecamp, was being built.

When a young sloth leaves its mother, it often lives in the forest near her, but she doesn't take care of it anymore.

Wildlife care specialist Katie carried Tornero into his new habitat. He looked around and climbed on a branch. Katie stayed with him until late in the evening, feeding him special treats and holding him. When Tornero snuggled into a hammock and fell asleep, Katie went home.

Early the next morning, the wildlife care specialists checked on Tornero, who calmly stretched and then yawned. His first night away from his mom had gone well.

Construction on Xena's new home, Wildlife Explorers Basecamp, was underway. But the wildlife care team got word that construction activities would be close to Tornero's home for a little while. So, the team decided to take Tornero and other animal ambassadors on an adventure to live for a short time at the Zoo hospital across the canyon.

Smokey

Einstein

Annie

Tornero's wildlife neighbors included his grandpa Nico the sloth, Smokey the opossum, Einstein the eagle owl, and Annie and Cheyenne the lynx kittens. Tornero was used to new people and places, so he was relaxed and comfortable during his stay at the hospital. While there, he learned to come when the wildlife care specialists called his name, and he practiced his climbing skills.

When things were back to normal at Wegeforth Bowl, Tornero and the other animals moved back home.

Introducing Tornero!

When Tornero was seven months old, the wildlife care specialists took him to an area on the Zoo's front plaza to help him practice being around larger groups of people. Tornero clung to a pillow while caregiver Julia introduced him to the Zoo's visitors, who were very excited to see him. Then she placed him on a special perch that was made of branches. Julia explained that Tornero was just learning to use the perch, which is why he laid on top of the branch instead of hanging from it.

Tornero was becoming more independent and soon wouldn't need to cling to a plush or a pillow anymore.

When Julia overheard a little boy ask his mother if he could have a sloth as a pet, she let everyone know that sloths are wild animals and they don't make good pets. She said that the Zoo's sloth ambassadors are there to help people learn about sloths and why we need to protect their rainforest homes.

As Tornero grew larger and stronger,
he learned to hang upside down on his perch.
He became very flexible—sometimes when he climbed, it looked like
he was doing the splits! Zoo visitors enjoyed seeing Tornero's natural
behaviors, especially because he moved in slow motion.

Tornero went through a growth spurt where he ate more and
pooped more, too! Even though sloths usually poop just once a week,
Tornero was pooping twice a week, and always in the same spot!

In addition to broccoli, Tornero ate cauliflower, spinach, kale, and jicama. Hibiscus flowers were a special treat for him. He preferred eating red and pink hibiscus but would munch on a yellow flower if the other colors weren't available. Tornero ate the stamen—or center stalk—of the flower first, followed by the petals and leaves. Sometimes, the pollen from the stamen left a "pollen mustache" under his nose.

Tornero chews with his mouth open. Once in a while, he falls asleep in the middle of a chew!

A Sloth Superstar!

Tornero is all grown up now and weighs 18 pounds. He looks like his mom, Xena, and he has long, shaggy blond hair like his sloth dad, Brad Pitt. Tornero lives in his comfortable sloth sanctuary with plenty of room to climb and hang out when he's not out with his caregivers, making special appearances for children and adults.

As one of
the most popular
wildlife ambassadors at
the San Diego Zoo, Tornero
touches the heart of everyone who
meets him. He also inspires people to care
about sloths, other wildlife, and their rainforest habitat.
Tornero is now a two-toed sloth superstar!

Fun Facts about Sloths

Sloths can do everything upside down: eat, sleep, and even have babies!

Two-toed sloths have two toes with claws on their front feet and three toes on their back feet.

There are six species, or types, of sloths.

LINNAEUS'S

HOFFMANN'S

To move to a new area of trees, sloths will often wait for the forest to flood and then swim to their next home.

Sloths spend almost all of their time in the trees.

Sloths are good swimmers.

With their low-energy diet of mostly leaves, sloths move slowly and sleep most of the day.

Sloths aren't lazy. They're just slow!

Three-toed sloths have three toes on their front and back feet.

BROWN-THROATED

PYGMY

PALE-THROATED

MANED

Sloths' fur collects algae which can give them a greenish tint, helping them blend into the trees.

A sloth's fur grows upward from its belly to its back, allowing water to run off when it's hanging upside down.

A sloth uses its long, curved claws to hang from branches.

Where Sloths Live in the World

Caribbean Sea

AFRICA

LINNAEUS'S SLOTHS' HABITAT

SLOTHS' HABITAT

Atlantic Ocean

SOUTH AMERICA

Pacific Ocean

PYGMY AND MANED THREE-TOED SLOTHS FACE EXTINCTION IN THEIR WILD HABITATS.

Threats to Wild Sloths:

- Loss of habitat, including cutting down rainforests for logging, farming, grazing, and urban areas.

- Harmful tourism activities in countries where sloths live, such as taking photos with young sloths, which are often taken from their mothers in the wild.

- Being killed by motor vehicles and attacked by dogs: when their habitat is broken up by roads, farms, and towns, sloths are forced to travel on the ground to get from one forest area to another.

- Being electrocuted on power lines.

How You Can Help

To learn how you can be an ally for sloths
and other wildlife as well as help the
San Diego Zoo Wildlife Alliance create a
world where all life thrives, visit
sdzwa.org

Special Note

Xena recently had another baby.
They live at the San Diego Zoo in
Wildlife Explorers Basecamp,
which is now open.

Ten Things You and Your Family Can Do to Help Wildlife:

1. Learn about the local wildlife that lives in or near your community.

2. Create your own wildlife habitat by planting native bushes, flowers, and trees in your yard. You can put up a bird feeder, too.

3. Keep your cats indoors so they stay safe and don't hurt local wildlife, such as birds, lizards, and small mammals.

4. Tell your friends and family not to purchase products made from threatened trees and plants, marine organisms, or wild animals when traveling abroad.

5. Put trash that can't be recycled in a garbage can so it doesn't end up harming wildlife or traveling to the ocean.

6. Recycle paper products, glass bottles, cans, and plastic, and say "no" to plastic bottles, straws, lids, and cutlery.

7. Use a reusable water bottle.

8. Take your own reusable bags to the grocery store.

9. Volunteer to be a "citizen scientist" on **wildwatchkenya.org** and **wildwatchburrowingowl.org** to help scientists identify wildlife in photos taken on trail cameras (with your parents' permission).

10. Find out more about how climate change is affecting our planet and share this information with the people in your life.